# HOW DOES GOD GUIDE US?

**Booklets from *Alpha—Questions of Life* include:**

*Is There More to Life Than This?*
*Who Is Jesus?*
*Why Did Jesus Die?*
*How Can We Have Faith?*
*Why and How Do I Pray?*
*Why and How Should I Read the Bible?*
*How Does God Guide Us?*
*The Holy Spirit*
*How Can I Resist Evil?*
*Why and How Should We Tell Others?*
*Does God Heal Today?*
*What about the Church?*
*How Can I Make the Most of the Rest of My Life?*

**Booklets from *Searching Issues* include:**

*Why Does God Allow Suffering?*
*What about Other Religions?*
*Is There Anything Wrong with Sex before Marriage?*
*How Does the New Age Movement Relate to Christianity?*
*What Is the Christian Attitude toward Homosexuality?*
*Is There a Conflict between Science and Christianity?*
*Is the Trinity Unbiblical, Unbelievable, and Irrelevant?*

# HOW DOES
# GOD GUIDE US?

NICKY GUMBEL

## *Alpha*

Alpha Resources
Alpha North America

Published in North America by Alpha North America
2275 Half Day Road, Suite 185, Deerfield, IL 60015

First published in 1993 as part of *Alpha—Questions of Life*. This
edition issued by special arrangement with KINGSWAY
COMMUNICATIONS LTD, Lottbridge Drove, Eastbourne
BN23 6NT, England

*How Does God Guide Us?*
by Nicky Gumbel

First printed by Alpha North America in 2007

Printed in the United States of America

Illustrations by Charlie Mackesy
Cover artwork by Glenn Andrews

ISBN 978-1-934564-15-8

1 2 3 4 5 6 7 8 9 10 Printing/Year 11 10 09 08 07

# Contents

# How Does God Guide Us?

We all have to make decisions in life. We are faced with decisions about relationships, marriage, children, use of time, jobs, homes, money, holidays, possessions, giving, and so on. Some of these are very big decisions, some smaller. In many cases, it is of the utmost importance that we make the right decisions—for instance in our choice of a marriage partner. We need God's help.

Guidance springs out of our relationship with God. He promises to guide those who are walking with Him.

He says, "I will instruct you and teach you in the way you should go" (Psalm 32:8). Jesus promises to lead and guide His followers: "He calls his own sheep by name and leads them out . . . His sheep follow him because they know his voice" (John 10:3, 4). He longs for us to discover His will (Colossians 1:9; Ephesians 5:17). He is concerned about each of us as individuals. He loves us and wants to speak to us about what we should be doing with our lives—about little things as well as big things.

God has a plan for our lives (Ephesians 2:10). Sometimes people are worried by this. They think, "I'm not sure that I want God's plan for my life. Will God's plans be good?" We need not fear. God loves us and wants the very best for our lives. Paul tells us that God's will for our lives is "good, pleasing and perfect"(Romans 12:2). He said to His people through the prophet Jeremiah, "'For I know the plans I have for you,' declares the Lord, 'plans to prosper you and not to harm you, plans to give you hope and a future'" (Jeremiah 29:11).

God is saying, "Don't you realize that I have a really good plan for your life? I have prepared something wonderful." This cry from the Lord's heart came because He saw the mess His people had gotten themselves into when they didn't follow His plans. All around us we see people whose lives are in a muddle. Often people say to me after they have come to Christ, "I wish I had become a Christian five or ten years earlier. Look at my life now. It is such a mess."

If we are to find out about God's plans for us, we

need to ask Him about them. God warned His people about embarking on plans without consulting Him: "'Woe to the obstinate children,' declares the Lord, 'to those who carry out plans that are not mine . . . who go down to Egypt *without consulting me* '" (Isaiah 30:1, 2, italics mine). Of course, Jesus is the supreme example of doing the will of His Father. He was consistently "led by the Spirit" (Luke 4:1) and only did what He saw His Father doing (John 5:19).

We make mistakes because we fail to consult the Lord. We make some plan and think, "I want to do that, but I am not quite sure whether God wants me to do it. I think I'd better not ask Him, just in case it's not His will for me!"

God guides us when we are prepared to do His will rather than insisting that our own way is right. The psalmist says, "He guides the humble" (Psalm 25:9) and "confides in those who fear [respect] him" (vs. 14). God guides those whose attitude is like Mary's: "I am the Lord's servant, and I am willing to do whatever he wants" (Luke 1:38, *The Living Bible*). The moment we are prepared to do His will, He begins to reveal His plans for our lives.

I go back to a verse in the Psalms time and time again: "Commit your way to the Lord; trust in him, and he will act" (Psalm 37:5, *Revised Standard Version*). Our part is to commit the decision to the Lord and then to trust Him. When we have done that, we can wait expectantly for Him to act.

Towards the end of our time in college, one of my friends named Nicky, who had become a Christian about the same time that I did, began to get to know very well a girl who was not a Christian. He felt it was not right to marry her unless she shared his faith in Christ. He did not want to put her under any pressure. So he did what the psalmist said and committed it to the Lord. He said, in effect, "Lord, if this relationship is not right, I pray that You will stop it. If it is right, then I pray she will become a Christian by the last day of the spring term." He did not tell her or anyone else about this date. He put his trust in God and waited for Him to act. The final day of the spring term arrived, and they went to a party together that night. Just before midnight she told him she wanted to go for a drive. So they got into the car and she gave him a whole string of directions out of the top of her head, just for fun: "Three left turns, three right turns, drive straight for three miles and stop." He played along and followed them. They ended up in the American cemetery, which has one enormous cross in the center surrounded by hundreds of little crosses. She was shocked and deeply moved by the symbol of the cross, and also by the fact that God had used her instructions to get her attention. She burst into tears. Moments later, she came to faith in Christ. They have now been happily married for many years and still look back and remember how God's hand was on them at that moment.

Given that we are willing to do what God wants us to do, in what ways should we expect God to speak to us? God guides us in various ways. Sometimes God speaks through one of the ways set out below;

sometimes it is a combination. If it is a major decision He may speak through all of them. They are sometimes called the five "C Ss."

## COMMANDING SCRIPTURE

As we have seen, God's general will for all people in all places in all circumstances is revealed in Scripture. He has told us what He thinks about a whole range of issues. From the Bible we know that certain things are wrong; we can be quite sure that God will not guide us to do these things. Sometimes a married person says, "I have fallen in love with this person. We love each other so much. I feel God is leading me to leave my spouse and to start this new relationship." But God has already made His will clear. He has said, "You shall not commit adultery" (Exodus 20:14). We can be quite sure that God will not guide us to commit adultery.

Sometimes people feel led to save money by not paying their income tax! But God has made it clear that we are to pay any taxes that are due (Romans 13:7). In these and many other areas God has revealed His general will. We do not need to ask His guidance; He has already given it. If we are not sure whether the Bible says anything on an issue, we may need to ask someone who knows the Bible better than we do. Once we have discovered what the Bible says, we need search no further.

Although God's general will is revealed in the Bible, we cannot always find His particular will for our lives there. As we have seen, the Bible tells us that it is His general will for people to get married. Although singleness is a high calling, it is the exception rather than the rule (see 1 Corinthians 7:2). We know that Christians are only free to marry other Christians (2 Corinthians 6:14). But the Bible does not tell us whom we should marry!

As we saw in the chapter on the Bible, God still speaks today through the Scriptures. He may speak to us as we read. The psalmist says, "Your statutes . . . are my counselors" (Psalm 119:24). That is not to say that we find God's will by opening the Bible anywhere at random and seeing what it says. Rather, as we develop the habit of regular, methodical Bible study we begin to find it quite extraordinary how appropriate each day's reading seems to be for the particular circumstances in which we find ourselves.

Sometimes a verse seems almost to leap off of the page at us, and we sense God speaking through it. This was certainly my experience, for example, when I sensed God calling me to change jobs. Each time I felt God speaking to me as I read the Bible, I wrote it down. I noted at least fifteen different occasions when I believe God spoke to me through the Bible about His call to me to leave my work as a lawyer and train for ordination in the Church of England.

## COMPELLING SPIRIT

Guidance is very personal. When we become Christians, the Spirit of God comes to live within us.

When He does so, He begins to communicate with us. We need to learn to hear His voice. Jesus said that His sheep (His followers) would recognize His voice (John 10:4, 5). We recognize a good friend's voice immediately on the telephone. If we do not know the person so well, it may be harder and take more time. The more we get to know Jesus, the easier we will find it to recognize His voice.

We find Paul and his companions, for example, planning to enter Bithynia, "but the Spirit of Jesus would not allow them to" (Acts 16:7). So they went a different way. We do not know how exactly the Spirit spoke to them, but it may have been in one of a number of ways.

Here are three examples of the way in which God speaks by His Spirit.

## Often God speaks to us when we pray

Prayer is a two-way conversation. Suppose I go to the doctor and say, "Doctor, I have a number of problems: I have a problem of fungus growing under my toenails, I have hemorrhoids, my eyes itch, I need a flu shot, I have very bad backaches, and I have tennis elbow." Then, having got through my list of complaints, I look at my watch and say, "Goodness me, time is getting on. Well, I must be off. Thanks very much for listening." The doctor might want to say, "Hang on a second. Why don't you listen to me?" If whenever we pray we only speak to God and never take time to listen, we make the same mistake. In the Bible we find God speaking to

His people. For example, on one occasion as the Christians were worshipping the Lord and fasting, the Holy Spirit said, "'Set apart for me Barnabas and Saul for the work to which I have called them.' So after they had fasted and prayed, they placed their hands on them and sent them off" (Acts 13:2, 3).

Again, we don't know exactly how the Holy Spirit spoke. It may be that as they were praying the thought came into their minds. That is a common way in which God speaks. People sometimes describe it as "impressions" or feeling it "in their bones." It is possible for the Holy Spirit to speak in all these ways.

Obviously such thoughts and feelings need to be tested (1 John 4:1). Is it in line with the Bible? Does it promote love? If it does not, it cannot come from a God who is love (1 John 4:16). Is it strengthening, encouraging, and comforting (1 Corinthians 14:3)? When we have made the decision, do we know God's peace (Colossians 3:15)?

## God sometimes speaks to us by giving us a strong desire to do something

"God . . . works in you to *will* and to act according to his good purpose" (Philippians 2:13, italics mine). As we surrender our wills to God, He works in us and often changes our desires. Again, I can speak from my own experience. Before I became a Christian, the last thing in the world I would have wanted to be was an ordained clergyman in the Church of England. Yet when I came to Christ and said I was willing to do what

He wanted, I found my desires changed. Now I cannot imagine a greater privilege or a more fulfilling job for me than the one I am doing at the moment.

Sometimes people try to imagine the thing that they would least like to do and then assume that God will ask them to do exactly that. I do not believe God is like that. So don't be frightened and say, "If I become a Christian, God will make me be a missionary." If that is what He wants you to do, and your will is surrendered, He will give you a strong desire to do that.

## God sometimes guides in more unusual ways

The Bible has many examples of God guiding individuals in dramatic ways. He spoke to Samuel as a small boy in a way in which he could hear with his physical ears (1 Samuel 3:4-14). He guided Abraham (Genesis 18), Joseph (Matthew 2:19), and Peter (Acts 12:7) through angels. He often spoke through prophets both in the Old Testament and in the New Testament (for instance, Agabus in Acts 11:27, 28;

21:10, 11). He guided through visions (sometimes referred to today as "pictures"). For example, one night God spoke to Paul in a vision. Paul saw a man in Macedonia standing and begging him, "Come over to Macedonia and help us." Not surprisingly, Paul and his companions took this as guidance that God had called them to preach the gospel in Macedonia (Acts 16:9, 10).

We also find examples of God guiding through dreams (for instance, Matthew 1:20; 2:12, 13, 22). I was praying for a couple who were good friends of ours. The husband had recently come to faith in Christ. The wife was highly intelligent but strongly against what had happened to her husband. She became a little hostile towards us. One night I had a dream in which I saw her face quite changed, her eyes full of the joy of the Lord. This encouraged us to continue praying and keeping close to them. A few months later she came to faith in Christ. I remember looking at her and seeing the face I had seen in the dream a few months earlier.

All these are ways in which God guided people in the past and still does today.

## COMMON SENSE

When we become Christians we are not called to abandon common sense. The psalmist warns: "Do not be like the horse or the mule, which have no understanding but must be controlled by bit and bridle or they will not come to you" (Psalm 32:9). The New Testament writers often encourage us to think and never discourage us from using our minds (for instance, 2 Timothy 2:7).

If we abandon common sense, then we get ourselves into absurd situations. In his book *Knowing God*, J. I. Packer quotes an example of a woman who each morning, having consecrated the day to the Lord as soon as she woke, "would then ask him whether she was to get up or not," and would not stir till "the voice" told her to dress.

> As she put on each article she asked the Lord whether she was to put it on and very often the Lord would tell her to put on the right shoe and leave off the other; sometimes she was to put on both stockings and no shoes; and sometimes both shoes and no stockings. It was the same with all the articles of dress.

It is true to say that God's promises of guidance were not given so that we could avoid the strain of thinking. Indeed, John Wesley, the father of Methodism, said that God *usually* guided him by presenting reasons to his mind for acting in a certain way. This is important in every area—especially in the areas of marriage and jobs.

Common sense is one of the factors to be taken into account in the whole area of choosing a partner for life. It is common sense to look at at least three very important areas.

*Spiritual compatibility.* Paul warns of the danger of

marrying someone who is not a Christian (2 Corinthians 6:14). In practice, if one of the parties is not a Christian, it nearly always leads to a great tension in the marriage. The Christian feels torn between a desire to serve his or her partner and a desire to serve the Lord. But spiritual compatibility means more than the fact that both are Christians. It means that each party respects the other's spirituality, rather than simply being able to say, "At least they pass the test of being a Christian."

*Personal compatibility.* Obviously, our marriage partner should be a very good friend and someone with whom there is a great deal in common. One of the many advantages of not sleeping together before getting married is that it is easier to concentrate on this area and discover whether or not there is personal compatibility. Often the sexual side can dominate the early stages of a relationship. If the foundations have not been built on friendship, then when the initial sexual excitement wears off it can leave the relationship with a very fragile basis.

*Physical compatibility.* By physical compatibility I mean we should be attracted to each other. It is not enough to be spiritually and emotionally compatible; the chemistry must work as well. Often the secular world puts it first, but this comes last in the order of priorities. The world often says that it is necessary to sleep together in order to see whether there is sexual compatibility. This is quite wrong. In the biological sense, any incompatibility that can be tested by sexual intercourse is so rare that it can be discounted.

*Again, common sense is vital when considering God's guidance about our jobs and careers.* The general rule is that we should stay with the job we are already in until God calls us to do something else (1 Corinthians 7:17-24). Having said that, in seeking God's will for one's career, it is common sense to take a long-term view of life. It is wise to look ahead ten, fifteen, twenty years and ask the questions: "Where is my present job taking me? Is that where I want to go in the long term? Or is my long-term vision for something quite different? In which case, where should I be now in order to get there?"

## COUNSEL OF THE SAINTS

The Book of Proverbs is full of injunctions to seek wise advice. The writer asserts that "a wise man listens to advice" (Proverbs 12:15). He warns that "plans fail for lack of counsel," but on the other hand, "with many advisers they succeed" (Proverbs 15:22). Therefore, he urges, "Make plans by seeking advice" (Proverbs 20:18).

While seeking advice is very important, we need to remember that ultimately our decisions are between us and God. They are our responsibility. We cannot shift that responsibility onto others or seek to blame them if things go wrong.

"Saints" is a New Testament way of describing all Christians (Philippians 1:1). "The counsel of the saints" is part of guidance—but it is not the only part. Sometimes it may be right to go ahead in spite of the advice of others.

If we are faced with a decision where we need advice, whom should we consult? To the writer of Proverbs, "fear of the Lord is the beginning of wisdom" (Proverbs 9:10). Presumably, therefore, he is thinking of advice from those who "fear the Lord." The best advisors are usually godly Christian people with wisdom and experience whom we respect. (It is also wise to seek the advice of parents whom we are to honor, even if we are past the age of being under their authority. Even if they are not Christians, they know us very well and can often have important insights into situations.)

I have found it a real help throughout my Christian life to have someone who is a mature Christian whom I respect and to whom I can go for advice on a whole range of issues. This has been different people at different times. I am so grateful to God for their wisdom and help in many areas. Often God's insight has come as we talked through the issues together.

When it comes to bigger decisions, I have found it helpful to seek a range of advice. Over the question of ordination I sought the advice of my parents, my two closest friends, my pastor, and those who were involved in the official process of selection.

The people whom we ask for advice should not be chosen on the basis that they will agree with what we have already planned to do! Sometimes one sees a person consulting countless people in the hope that he or she will eventually find somebody who will endorse their plans. Such advice has little weight and simply enables the person to say, "And I consulted this person and he or she agreed."

We should consult people on the basis of their spiritual authority or their relationship to us, regardless of what we may anticipate their views to be. When my friends, Nicky and Sila Lee, who now minister in a church in central London, became Christians, they wondered whether it was right to continue their relationship, because although they were very much in love they were still so young and had no immediate prospects of marriage.

Nicky talked to a very wise Christian man for whom he had great respect. Nicky knew the man had firm views on the subject of relationships and that he felt it was unwise to be too deeply involved while still in college. Nevertheless, Nicky decided to consult him.

The man asked Nicky, "Have you committed your relationship with Sila to the Lord?" Nicky replied with some hesitation and great honesty, "I think I have, but sometimes I am not sure," to which this wise man replied, "I can see that you love her. I think you should continue in your relationship with her." Because this advice came from a surprising source it carried additional weight. The advice was very good, and they have now had many years of happily married life to prove it.

# CIRCUMSTANTIAL SIGNS

God is in ultimate control of all events; the writer of Proverbs points out: "In his heart a man plans his course, but the Lord determines his steps" (Proverbs 16:9). Sometimes God opens doors (1 Corinthians 16:9,) and sometimes He closes them (Acts 16:7).

On two occasions in my life God has closed the door on something that I very much wanted, and which I believed at the time was God's will. I tried to force the doors open. I prayed and I struggled and I fought, but they would not open. On both occasions I was bitterly disappointed. But I understand now, years later, why God closed those doors. Indeed I am grateful that He did. However, I am not sure we will ever know this side of heaven why God has closed certain doors in our lives.

Sometimes God opens doors in a remarkable way. The circumstances and the timing point clearly to the hand of God (for instance, Genesis 24). Michael Bourdeaux is head of Keston College, a research unit devoted to helping believers in what were communist lands. His work and research are respected by governments all over the world. He studied Russian at Oxford and his Russian teacher, Dr. Zernov, sent him a letter he had received because he thought it would interest him. It detailed how monks were beaten up by the KGB and subjected to inhuman medical examinations; how they were being rounded up in trucks and dumped many hundreds of miles away. The letter was written very simply, with no adornment, and as he read it Michael Bourdeaux felt he was hearing the true voice of the persecuted church. The letter was signed Varavva and Pronina.

In August 1964, Michael went on a trip to Moscow, and on his first evening there met up with old friends who detailed how the persecutions were getting worse. In particular the old church of St. Peter and St. Paul had been demolished. They suggested that he go and see it for himself.

So he took a taxi and arrived at dusk. When he came to the square where he had remembered a very beautiful church, he found nothing except a twelve-foot-high fence, which hid the rubble where the church had been. Over on the other side of the square, climbing the fence to try to see what was inside, were two women. He watched them, and when they finally left the square he followed them for a hundred yards and eventually caught up with them. They asked, "Who are you?" He replied, "I am a foreigner. I have come to find out what is happening here in the Soviet Union."

They took him back to the house of another woman who asked him why he had come. He said he had received a letter from the Ukraine via Paris. When she asked who it was from, he replied, "Varavva and Pronina." There was silence. He wondered if he had said something wrong. A flood of uncontrolled sobbing followed. The woman pointed and said, "This is Varavva, and this is Pronina."

The population of Russia is over one hundred forty million. The Ukraine, from where the letter was written, is over eight hundred miles from Moscow.

Michael Bourdeaux had flown from England six months after the letter had been written. He and the women would not have met had either party arrived at the demolished church an hour earlier or an hour later. That was one of the ways God called Michael Bourdeaux to set up his life's work.[1]

## Don't be in a hurry

Sometimes God's guidance seems to come immediately when it is asked for (for instance, Genesis 24), but often it takes much longer—sometimes months or even years. We may have a sense that God is going to do something in our lives but have to wait a long time for the fulfillment. On these occasions we need patience like that of Abraham who "after waiting patiently . . . received what was promised" (Hebrews 6:15). While waiting, he was tempted at one point to try and fulfill God's promises by his own means—with disastrous results (see Genesis 16 and 21).

Sometimes we hear God correctly, but we get the timing wrong. God spoke to Joseph in a dream about what would happen to him and his family. He probably expected immediate fulfillment, but he had to wait years. Indeed, while he was in prison it must have been hard for him to believe that his dreams would ever be fulfilled. But thirteen years after the original dream, he saw God's fulfillment. The waiting was part of the preparation (see Genesis 37–50).

In this area of guidance, we all make mistakes. Sometimes, like Abraham, we try to fulfill God's plans by our own wrong methods. Like Joseph we get the timing wrong. Sometimes we feel that we have made too much of a mess of our lives by the time we come to Christ for God to do anything with us. But God is greater than that. He is able to "restore to you the years which the swarming locust has eaten" (Joel 2:25, *Revised Standard Version*). He is able to make something good out of whatever is left of our lives—whether it is a short time or a long time—if we will offer what we have to Him and cooperate with His Spirit.

Lord Radstock was staying in a hotel in Norway in the mid-nineteenth century. He heard a little girl playing the piano down in the hallway. She was making a terrible noise: "Plink . . . plunk . . . plink . . . " It was driving him mad! A man came and sat beside her and began playing alongside her, filling in the gaps. The result was the most beautiful music. He later

discovered that the man playing alongside was the girl's father, Aleksandr Borodin, composer of the opera *Prince Igor.*

Paul writes that "in all things God works for the good of those who love him, who have been called according to his purpose" (Romans 8:28). As we falteringly play our part—seeking His will for our lives by reading (commanding Scripture), listening (controlling Spirit), thinking (common sense), talking (counsel of the saints), watching (circumstantial signs), and waiting—God comes and sits alongside us "and in all things . . . works for the good." He takes our plink, plunk, plink and makes something beautiful out of our lives.

# Notes

1. Michael Bordeaux, *Risen Indeed* (Dartman, Longmon Todd, 1983)

# Alpha

This book is an Alpha resource. The Alpha course is a practical introduction to the Christian faith initiated by Holy Trinity Brompton in London, and now being run by thousands of churches throughout the U.K., North America, and internationally.

For more information on Alpha, and details of available resources, please contact:

**Alpha U.S.A.**
2275 Half Day Road
Suite 185
Deerfield, IL 60015
Tel: 800.362.5742
Tel: + 212.406.5269
e-mail: info@alphausa.org
www.alphausa.org

**Alpha Canada**
Suite #230 – 11331 Coppersmith Way
Riverside Business Park
Richmond, BC V7A 5J9
Tel: 800.743.0899
Fax: 604.271.6124
e-mail: office@alphacanada.org
www.alphacanada.org

To purchase resources in Canada:

**David C. Cook Distribution Canada**
P.O. Box 98, 55 Woodslee Avenue
Paris, ONT N3L 3E5
Tel: 800.263.2664
Fax: 800.461.8575
e-mail: custserve@davidccook.ca
www.davidccook.ca

# Alpha Titles Available

*Why Jesus?*   A booklet given to all participants at the start of the Alpha course. "The clearest, best illustrated and most challenging short presentation of Jesus that I know." – Michael Green

*Why Christmas?*   The Christmas version of *Why Jesus?*

*Searching Issues*   The seven issues most often raised by participants on the Alpha course: suffering, other religions, sex before marriage, the New Age, homosexuality, science and Christianity, and the Trinity.

*A Life Worth Living*   What happens after Alpha? Based on the book of Philippians, this is an invaluable next step for those who have just completed the Alpha course, and for anyone eager to put their faith on a firm biblical footing.

*How to Run the Alpha Course: Telling Others*   The theological principles and the practical details of how courses are run.

*Challenging Lifestyle*   Studies in the Sermon on the Mount showing how Jesus' teaching flies in the face of modern lifestyle and presents us with a radical alternative.

*30 Days*   Nicky Gumbel selects thirty passages from the Old and New Testament which can be read over thirty days. It is designed for those on an Alpha course and others who are interested in beginning to explore the Bible.

*The Heart of Revival*   Ten Bible studies based on the book of Isaiah, drawing out important truths for today by interpreting some of the teaching of the Old Testament prophet Isaiah. The book seeks to understand what revival might mean and how we can prepare to be part of it.

*All titles are by Nicky Gumbel, who is Vicar of
Holy Trinity Brompton in London*